# SHOCKING CON TRICKS

**JONNY ZUCKER**

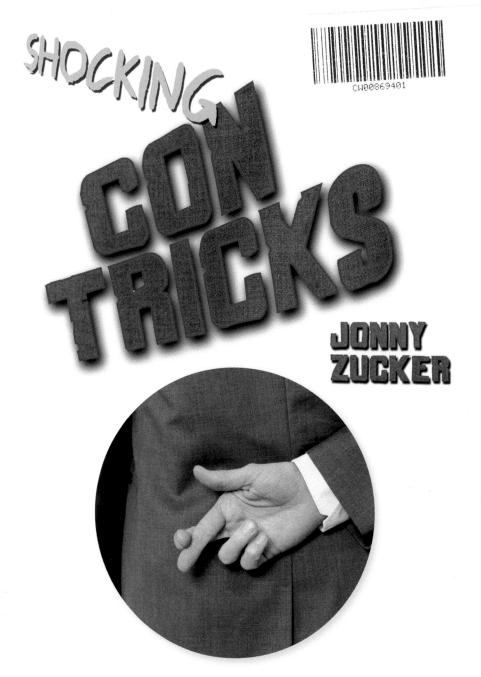

Badger Publishing Limited
Oldmedow Road,
Hardwick Industrial Estate,
King's Lynn PE30 4JJ
Telephone: 01438 791037

www.badgerlearning.co.uk

4 6 8 10 9 7 5

Shocking Con Tricks ISBN 978-1-78464-107-8

Publisher: Susan Ross
Senior Editor: Danny Pearson
Publishing Assistant: Claire Morgan
Designer: Fiona Grant
Series Consultant: Dee Reid

Photos: Cover Image: © fStop Images GmbH/Alamy
Page 5: Steve Meddle/REX
Page 6: Stock Connection/REX
Page 9: © Charles O. Cecil / Alamy
Page 11: Everett Collection/REX
Page 12: David Rose/The Independent/REX
Page 13: Tophams/Topham Picturepoint/Press Association Images
Page 14: Associated Newspapers /REX
Page 16: REX
Page 17: © CBW/Alamy
Page 18: © INTERFOTO/Alamy
Page 19: Kypros/REX
Page 21: © Will Stanton/Alamy
Page 22: KPA/Zuma/REX
Page 23: Julian Simmonds/REX
Page 25: © Eye Candy Images/Alamy
Page 26: © Philip Bramhill/Alamy
Page 27: © RayArt Graphics/Alamy
Page 30: © Gergely Kishonthy/Alamy

Attempts to contact all copyright holders have been made.
If any omitted would care to contact Badger Learning, we will be happy to make appropriate arrangements.

# Contents

# Vocabulary

| | |
|---|---|
| collapsing | surprisingly |
| confidence | tollbooths |
| embarrassed | valuable |
| investors | wealthy |

# 1. THE CON BEGINS

**The con set up**

People have been cheating each other for centuries but the word 'con' first appeared around a hundred and fifty years ago.

A con happens when a 'con man' or 'con woman' selects a 'mark' or a victim and cheats them out of money or valuables, by lying and playing a trick on them.

In 1849, a New Yorker called William Thompson walked up to smartly-dressed strangers and asked them, "Do you have the confidence to lend me your watch until tomorrow?"

Surprisingly, lots of people did! They handed over their gold watches and then he disappeared into the crowds.

Of course, they never saw their watches again! They had been truly conned.

Later that year, a man who had already handed over his watch to Thompson a few weeks before, saw him trying to con someone else.

The police were called and Thompson was arrested. The story was reported in newspapers across the country.

The media called Thompson 'the confidence man'.

Thompson's story inspired Herman Melville's novel *The Confidence-Man*. It was first published on April Fool's day!

## The great diamond hoax

In 1871, Philip Arnold and John Slack, who were cousins, bought a bag of cheap diamonds and buried them in a field in Wyoming.

This is known as 'salting'.

They travelled to San Francisco, nearly 1000 miles away, and invited some businessmen to come and see their 'diamond field'.

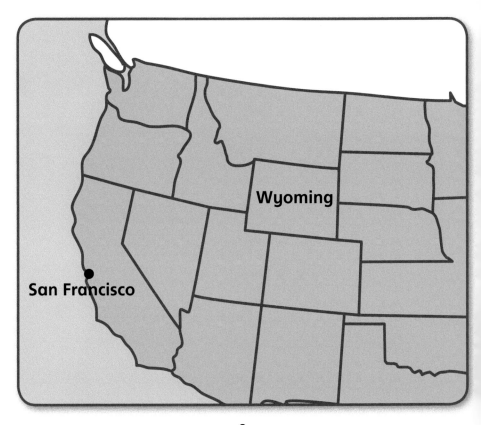

The men thought it might be a con so they brought diamond experts with them.

The experts looked at the diamonds Arnold and Slack had buried and thought it was a real diamond field.

The men paid Arnold and Slack $660,000 dollars, which was a huge amount of money in those days.

After the sale, another expert visited the field and said that it was a con. The men tried to get their money back from Arnold and Slack but they didn't get it all.

## Brooklyn Bridge for sale

George Parker was a con man. In the 1880s, he 'sold' the Brooklyn Bridge not once, not twice, but over and over again.

His con was simple:

He picked out 'marks' who had not been living in America very long and who did not speak English very well.

He told them he owned Brooklyn Bridge. He said he needed to make some money quickly so he was selling it for a very low price.

Then he showed them lots of drawings and important-looking papers about the bridge.

He told them that they could make lots of money by setting up tollbooths and charging people to cross the bridge.

A surprising number of people fell for this scam.

The New York police made lots of people take down tollbooths they had set up.

WOW! facts

George Parker spent the last eight years of his life in prison, where he entertained other prisoners with tales of his con tricks.

**How much is that tower?**
In 1925, con man Victor Lustig
started telling people that
he worked for the French
Government. He also
told them that he had been
chosen to sell the Eiffel Tower
in Paris as scrap metal.

The Eiffel Tower is 301 metres
tall. That's a lot of scrap metal!

Twelve people put in bids for the scrap metal.

Lustig chose the one who offered the most money – a businessman called Monsieur Poisson.

Poisson paid Lustig a lot of money and Lustig fled to Austria with a suitcase full of cash.

Poisson was so embarrassed that he didn't tell anyone what had happened.

# 2. THIS CON IS PERSONAL

Ferdinand Demara's con was to pretend he was trained to do different jobs when he wasn't trained at all.

He joined the navy and later taught at a college, but Demara's biggest con was pretending he was a doctor.

In 1951, he got a job on a Royal Canadian Navy ship. He had no idea how to do operations so he used to quickly read about them in medical books the night before.

He once saved the lives of 16 wounded Korean soldiers.

He even performed major heart surgery! And the most amazing thing? No one died after any of his operations.

Demara's last job was working in a prison. But the police caught up with him and he ended up staying in prison as a prisoner.

WOW! facts

When it was discovered that Demara was not a real doctor, the ship's captain refused to believe it because Demara had saved so many lives.

## The spy lie

In 1992, Robert Hendy-Freegard conned people into believing he was a spy for MI5, the British spy agency.

Then he told them that they were in danger and he asked them for money. He said he would use the money to protect them.

He told some people to stay hidden in their homes for weeks while he stole their money and cars.

He also told several women that he wanted to marry them but that he would need large sums of money before the wedding. Most of the women paid him large sums of cash.

But Scotland Yard and the FBI finally caught him.

One of his victim's mothers agreed to give him £10,000 but only if she met her at Heathrow Airport. When he got there the police grabbed him and his days of 'spying' were over.

### My Dad is a legend

In 1983, 19-year-old David Hampton was refused entry to a New York nightclub. So he told them that his father was the famous Hollywood actor, Sidney Poitier.

They believed him and he was let in to the nightclub and treated as a celebrity.

After that, Hampton began calling himself 'David Poitier' to get free meals in restaurants, and to get invited to famous people's houses.

Later that year Hampton was caught and sent to prison for 21 months.

Hampton    85-B-0075

# 3. TAKE, TAKE, TAKE

**The collapsing pyramid**

In 2008, a group of women in the south of England launched a scheme called 'Give and Take.'

This was called a pyramid con. How did it work?

Group A asks Group B to pay £3000 into the scheme. Group A takes most of that money.

Then Group B asks Group C to pay £3000 into the scheme. Group A takes half of that money and Group B keeps half the money.

Group D pays £3000 into the scheme and their money gets spread between the other groups. But it then gets harder and harder to get new groups to join so Groups D and E get little or no money.

The women who set up 'Give and Take' made £20 million but 90% of people further down the pyramid lost all their money.

WOW! facts

The women who set up 'Give and Take' were nearly 70 years of age and most of them were grandmothers! They were sent to prison for nine months.

The man who made off with the money

In the 'Give and Take' scam lots of people lost thousands of pounds. But Bernie Madoff's pyramid scam cost people billions of pounds.

In 1990, Madoff told people that if they gave him money he would invest it and make huge profits for them.

But Madoff didn't invest any of it. If someone asked for their original sum of money back plus their profits, he paid them with money given to him by newer investors in the scheme.

It is said that Madoff stole close to $65 billion and he was called 'The King of Thieves'.

In 2008, when Madoff was 74 years of age, he was given a 150-year prison sentence. He will spend the rest of his life in prison.

# 4. CLASSIC CONS

**The toy ploy**

In this con, a con man goes into a bar, sits down and puts a very old-looking toy on the seat beside him.

The toy looks valuable but, in fact, the con man has bought it cheaply.

Then the con man says he has to go out to make a call.

While he is out, the conman's 'shill' or assistant walks into the bar. He looks at the toy and gasps. He says the toy is worth hundreds of pounds and asks if he can buy it.

The barman explains that it's not his toy and so he can't sell it. The shill then leaves.

When the con man returns, the barman, who has heard the shill saying how valuable the toy was, is keen to pay a lot of money for the toy.

The con man accepts the cash and leaves with a grin on his face.

### The Spanish prisoner

This scam was first used over 400 years ago and it is still being used today.

First, the con man approaches a mark and pretends to have a cousin who is a very wealthy businessman. He tells the mark that this cousin is locked up in a Spanish prison because the Spanish police think that he is someone else.

Then the con man says the police will let the wealthy man go if a sum of money is paid to them.

The con man says that if the mark provides this sum, the wealthy businessman will pay the mark a very large sum of money to say thank you, when he is set free.

The mark hands over the cash, expecting to get the very large sum of money later on, but, of course, the con man is never seen again.

## The false mugging

How does this con work?

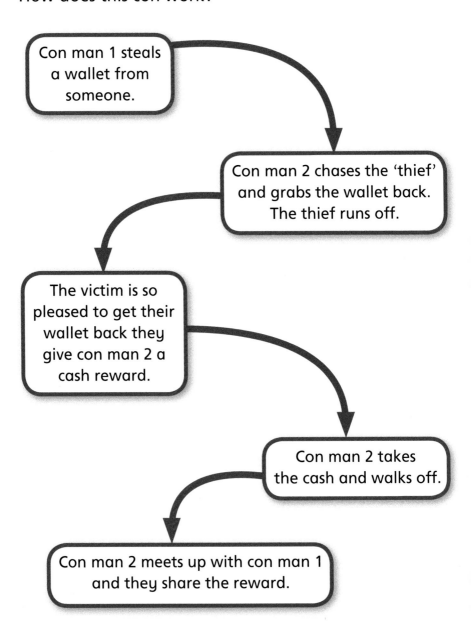

Con man 1 steals a wallet from someone.

Con man 2 chases the 'thief' and grabs the wallet back. The thief runs off.

The victim is so pleased to get their wallet back they give con man 2 a cash reward.

Con man 2 takes the cash and walks off.

Con man 2 meets up with con man 1 and they share the reward.

# The app scam

In 2008, a new app appeared on the Apple App Store.

There was no information about what the app could do, but it was called 'I AM RICH' and cost $599.99 which was the largest amount anyone was allowed to charge for an app in those days.

There was a lot of talk about it on websites and message boards.

People wondered if the app revealed a secret that could make you rich.

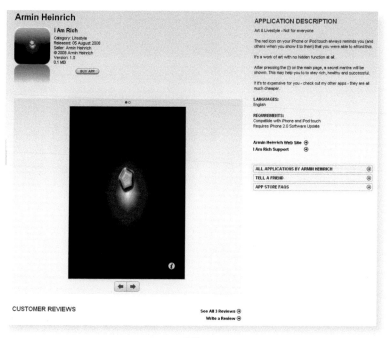

The app was on sale for just 24 hours and in that time eight people bought it.

When these buyers opened the app, all they got was a picture of a gleaming red gem in the middle of their screens!

**WOW! facts**

Two buyers asked for a refund but surprisingly the other six buyers kept the app. Maybe they were too embarrassed to admit they had been conned.

## Questions

What did the New York police have to do as a result of the Brooklyn Bridge scam? *(page 11)*

What did Victor Lustig try to sell? *(page 12)*

How did Ferdinand Demara manage to trick people into believing he was a doctor? *(page 14-15)*

How did Robert Hendy-Freegard con his victims? *(page 16-17)*

How many years in prison was Bernie Madoff sentenced to? *(page 23)*

Why do you think people fall for cons?

# INDEX